CAPRICORN

by Elizabeth Andrews

WELCOME TO DiscoverRoo!

This book is filled with videos, puzzles, games, and more! Scan the QR codes* while you read, or visit the website below to make this book pop.

popbooksonline.com/cap

abdobooks.com

Published by Pop!, a division of ABDO, PO Box 398166, Minneapolis, Minnesota 55439. Copyright © 2026 by Abdo Consulting Group, Inc. International copyrights reserved in all countries. No part of this book may be reproduced in any form without written permission from the publisher. DiscoverRoo™ is a trademark and logo of Pop!.

Printed in the United States of America, North Mankato, Minnesota.

042025
082025

THIS BOOK CONTAINS RECYCLED MATERIALS

Cover Photo: Splendoura Prints; Shutterstock Images
Interior Photos: Getty Images; Shutterstock Images; Wikimedia Commons
Editor: Tyler Gieseke
Series Designer: Laura Graphenteen

Library of Congress Control Number: 2024948398

Publisher's Cataloging-in-Publication Data
Names: Andrews, Elizabeth, author.
Title: Capricorn / by Elizabeth Andrews
Description: Minneapolis, Minnesota : Pop!, 2026 | Series: Zodiac signs | Includes online resources and index
Identifiers: ISBN 9781098247898 (lib. bdg.) | ISBN 9781098248437 (ebook)
Subjects: LCSH: Capricorn (Astrology)--Juvenile literature. | Goat (Astrology)--Juvenile literature. | Zodiac--Juvenile literature. | Astrology--Juvenile literature. | Astrology--Charts, diagrams, etc.--Juvenile literature.
Classification: DDC 133.52--dc23

*Scanning QR codes requires a web-enabled smart device with a QR code reader app and a camera.

TABLE OF CONTENTS

MEET THE CAPRICORN!

Capricorn is the tenth sign of the zodiac.

People with the Capricorn sign are born between December 22 and January 19.

When people ask for your "star sign," they are likely asking for your sun sign. This is the zodiac sign the sun appeared in at your birth.

Carnation

CAPRICORN

constellation
feminine
garnet
cardinal
SAT
numbers
2
8
symbol

ZODIAC CALENDAR

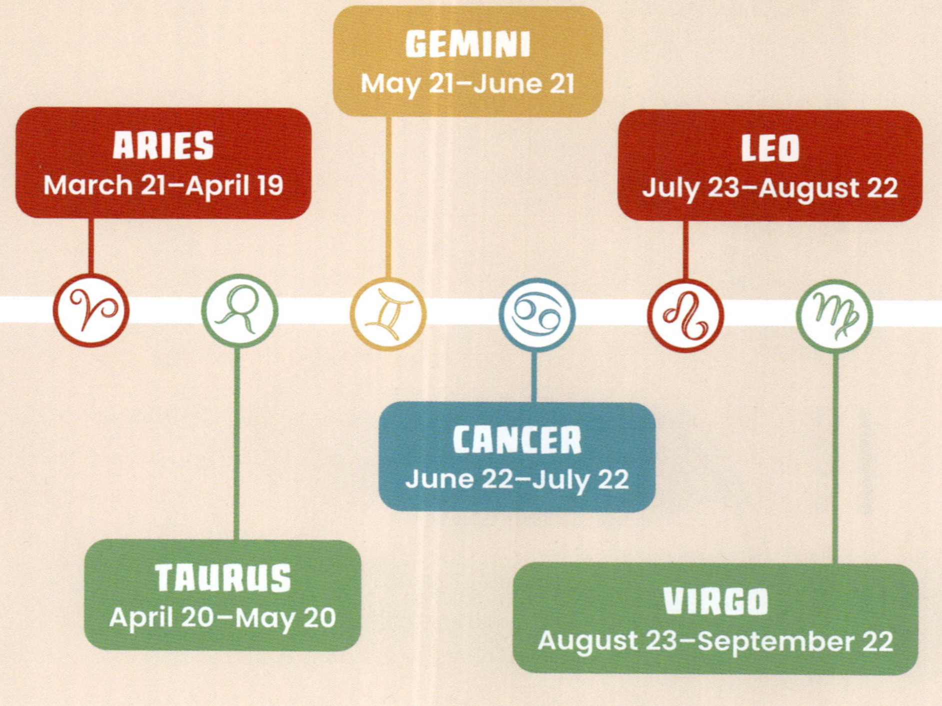

Three features help describe zodiac signs. Signs can be masculine or feminine. Each zodiac sign is given a mode. The three modes are cardinal, fixed, and mutable. Each zodiac is also

a fire, air, earth, or water sign. No zodiac signs share the same three features.

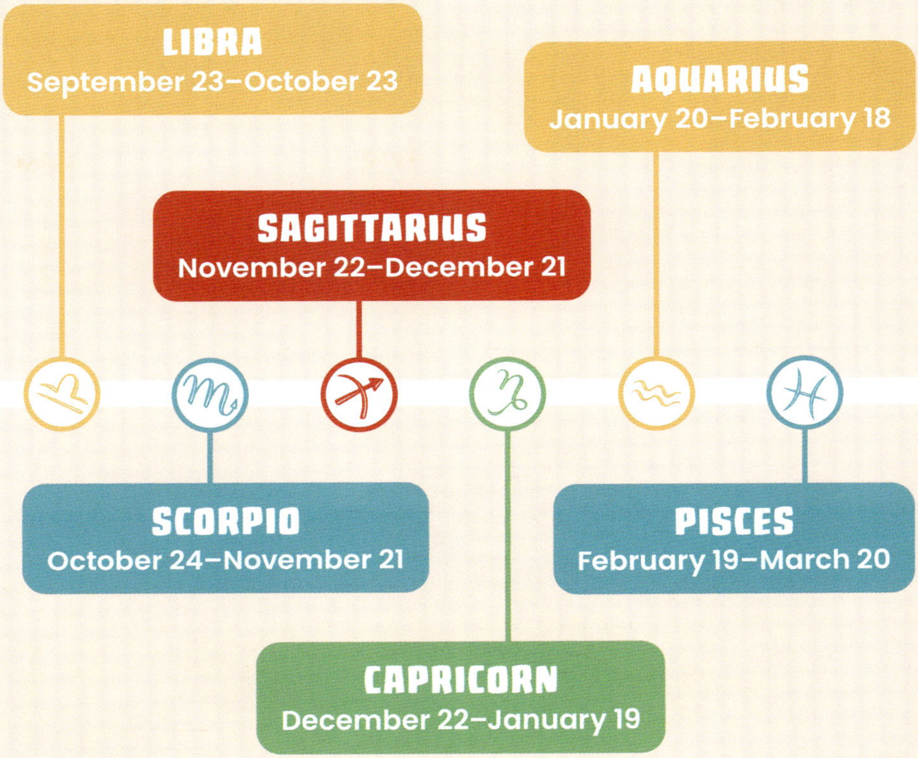

DID YOU KNOW? The **constellation** Capricorns were born under is called Capricornus.

Feminine signs might reflect on their emotions or daily life in journals.

Capricorn is a feminine, cardinal, earth sign. Feminine signs are grounded. Many of their actions are done **internally**. They are in touch with their own emotions and those around them.

Modes describe how signs interact with the outside world. Cardinal signs make things happen. They are quick to act when an idea strikes. Earth signs are often dependable people with lots of plans. They are honest, steady, and calm.

Pan was very connected to music. He created his own instrument, the panpipes!

Capricorns are **represented** by the goat. Like the goat, they are steady and can climb to great heights. Ancient Greeks connected their god Pan to the constellation Capricornus. Pan was half-goat and half-man. Once, when running from a monster, Pan jumped in a river and changed into a half-goat, half-fish. The king of the gods, Zeus, thought it was funny and put the picture in the stars.

In the Northern Hemisphere, the Capricornus constellation is visible from August to November. In the Southern Hemisphere, it is visible from June to October.

HISTORY OF ASTROLOGY

Humans have looked for life's **spiritual** meaning since the beginning of time. They often looked to the stars for this. Astrology is the practice of reading the movements of planets and other **celestial** bodies and connecting them to life on Earth.

Some ancient people used the zodiac signs to predict future events.

Babylonians invented the zodiac in Mesopotamia over 5,000 years ago. Mesopotamia was the first known civilization. Babylon was one of the region's largest cities.

Ptolemy was an Egyptian man who studied the stars.

The zodiac is a belt of space around Earth that has 12 well-known **constellations**. Ancient people noticed that the sun seemed to move in front of these constellations throughout a year. The sun spends about a month in each constellation.

The constellations in the zodiac belt are Aries, Taurus, Gemini, Cancer, Leo, Virgo, Libra, Scorpius, Sagittarius, Capricornus, Aquarius, and Pisces. Together they make up the 12 zodiac signs. They are all **represented** by different **symbols**.

Islamic astrologers created new ways to map and measure stars.

THE ZODIAC WHEEL

DID YOU KNOW?

Most zodiac symbols are animals. The ancient Greeks called the belt of space *zodiakos kyklos,* or "circle of animals."

CHAPTER 3

THE RESPONSIBLE FRIEND

Saturn rules the sign of Capricorn. Saturn is the planet of problems, limitations, **discipline**, and dependability. Capricorns are aware of the limits they face, such as, time, money, and location. Their awareness of such troubles leaves Capricorns believing they can depend only on themselves.

Capricorns prefer to handle any problems or projects on their own.

Some people say Capricorns are grown up by the time they are six. They can be very driven and dream of climbing to high places, just like the goat that **represents** them. Capricorns will chase their dreams with **determination**.

Capricorns are very reasonable. They like to know things. Their brains move quickly, and they can understand new subjects easily. Sometimes Capricorns can be too aware of the world and its problems. They may struggle to see the joy in everyday life.

Capricorns are the **responsible** friend of the zodiac. Their organization and planning make them great people to have around. Capricorns only open up to select, trusted people in their lives. They will stop at nothing to help those they care about. Capricorns like the security that comes with having close friends.

Greta Thunberg is a Capricorn. She has organized many ways for people to ask world leaders to protect the planet.

Capricorns can lean on their friends to keep from overthinking.

Capricorns have a good sense of humor. Only close friends get to see the goofy and fun side of a Capricorn. It may help all Capricorns to reconnect with the simple things that made them happy as young children.

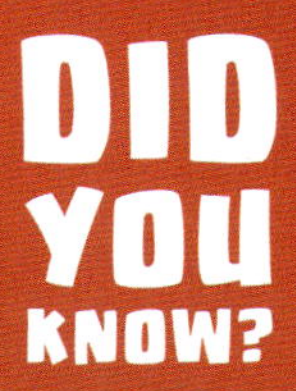

Capricorns might involve themselves in their friends' business because they think they know best.

BORN TO SUCCEED

Capricorns are the sign of **discipline**.

They are driven by their longing for success. Success can come from wealth, love, and positions of power. Capricorns won't let anything get in their way. They are very patient and will wait for the best opportunities to come up.

Garnet is the stone of Capricorns. It is the stone of fearlessness.

Lebron James (right) *is a Capricorn. He is one of the best basketball players of all time.*

Capricorns make good team captains.

Capricorns are careful with money. It connects to their need for security. They are good savers. Capricorns are likely to possess a lot of money. However, it won't be until later in their lives. They think before they spend money. Like most things in a Capricorn's life, money is handled carefully.

Capricorns want people to like them.

They want to be honored for their skills.

Some people view Capricorns as prideful.

They may also appear cold and reserved.

Other people enjoy how mysterious

Capricorns seem.

Capricorns like going outside and experiencing nature.

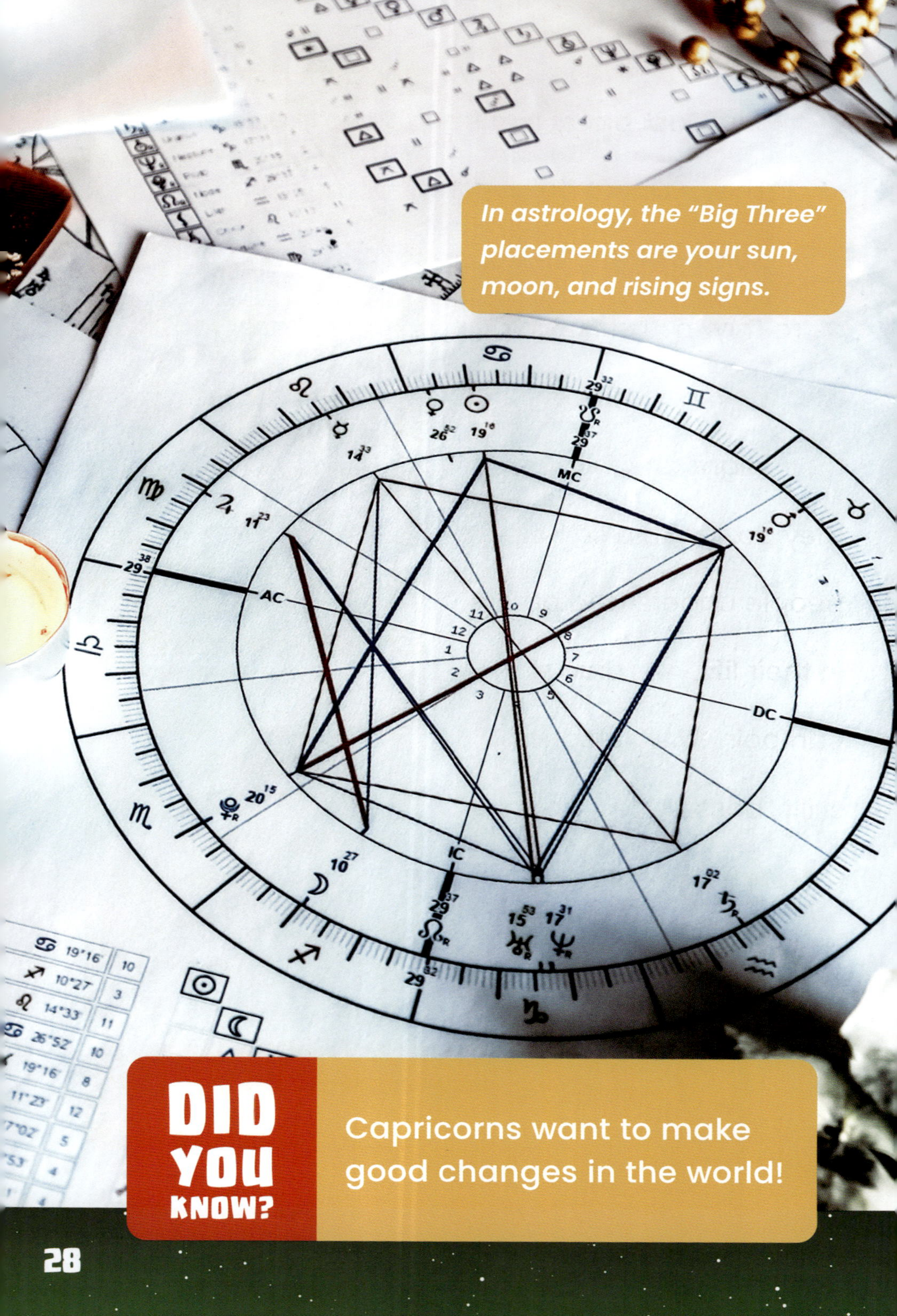

DID YOU KNOW?

Capricorns want to make good changes in the world!

Today, astrology can answer questions about an individual. People use astrology to understand who they are and why they might do what they do. It can also help people understand others in their life. A zodiac sign can point out personal skills, possibilities, and **internal motivations**.

WHAT IS A BIRTH CHART?

Each person's birth chart contains all the planets in our solar system, the moon, and the sun. The location of where each **celestial** body was based on the exact time and location of a person's birth can be marked on a birth chart. A birth chart can explain even more about a person than what only a sun sign can. The placement of each planet affects the drive of a person. This reveals personal motivations. Astrology experts can read birth charts.

TEXT-TO-SELF

Are you a Capricorn? If so, do you think the sign matches your personality? If not, what do you have in common with Capricorns?

TEXT-TO-TEXT

Have you read any books about the other zodiac signs? How were those signs similar to and different from Capricorn?

TEXT-TO-WORLD

With the help of an adult, look up famous Capricorns. Pick one person and write a few sentences about ways that person shows Capricorn qualities.

GLOSSARY

celestial — having to do with the sky or outer space.

constellation — a group of stars that forms a pattern.

determination — the quality of having a firm goal.

discipline — training that molds, corrects, or perfects something.

internal — of, relating to, or being on the inside.

motivation — something that makes one want to do something.

represent — to stand for or be a sign of.

responsible — able to make the right decisions.

spiritual — having to do with people's beliefs in things such as the soul, nature, and what happens after death.

symbol — an object or picture that represents something else.

INDEX

popbooksonline.com/cap

*Scanning QR codes requires a web-enabled smart device with a QR code reader app and a camera.